RIPPING OUT MY HEART

THE REAL FACE OF GRIEF

Jeanne Roy

bodyindependent

Arcadia, CA

The contents of this book include stories, situations, conversations, and information relying on the memory of the author alone. Any mistakes or misquoting are that of the author alone.

For permission requests, write to Jeanne Roy at
bodyindependent@gmail.com

Ripping Out My Heart / Jeanne Roy. —1st ed.
ISBN 979-8-218-41568-6

Also by the Author

SPIKE UP!
Becoming an Athlete at 60

In memory of my husband, Dean.
I wish I never had to write this.
You're still my cutman! Wut?

Author's Note

This is not a book about my husband's death, the how or the why, but to understand some of the things within, some context is required. My husband, Dean, went into the hospital on June 9, 2023. Until the morning of July 3, there was a light at the end of the tunnel. Actually, that morning there was still a light, only it was the light of a train coming straight at me. All I could do is hunker down and brace for impact. That impact came the afternoon of July 5, when Dean took his last breath. He was 66. I was 62. We'd been together for 32 years, married for 27. We had no children, no emotionally close family. Dean was a biomechanic body worker for people and horses. No one does what he did. He was a master of just about every martial art and a legend in the San Soo community. I am a former prosecutor turned athlete. Between us, we know many people and have many friends.

You may have noticed that I switch on and off between past and present tense. It isn't because I don't know the difference but because, even though Dean is dead, not everything is past. He still is a legend in the San Soo community; his friends are still his friends. We "had" no children but we "have" no children either. You see what I mean?

You will also notice that even though these thoughts apply to the death of a life partner or spouse of any sex, I usually use "husband" because, well, it was my husband who died and it would sound silly to refer to him as anything else.

Lastly, this book is written solely from my point of view at the time I first put the words to the page. I do not presume to think that everyone, or anyone, will feel or have felt the way that I do or did. You may even be offended at my characterization of certain things. Grief is solitary and we all experience it differently.

The first words of the first draft were written mid-October 2023 and comprise Memorialize This. The last words, which comprise One Track Mind II, were written the first week of January 2024. Advice came later, along with the Afterword. Other than editing so that my words, hopefully, make sense, I left the content as is. In other words, I didn't go back and make changes to reflect how I feel now nor did I soften or sanitize my words. I hope this helps.

The Why

As of this writing, my husband, Dean, died just short of 4 months ago. I didn't see it coming. No one did. I started keeping notes about things shortly after his death. I really didn't know why, I just knew that I needed to write them down. Some might call this "journaling" but when I look back at the notes, I was just really pissed off. The thought of turning my notes into a book didn't enter my mind until a couple of months after his death when it became clear that the "grief" books out there just weren't cutting it. The thought became reality after speaking with a friend whose husband had died about 4 years previous. She told me that I had to write this now while everything was still fresh and raw. She told me that it needed to be written because people need to know the reality of grief and not the sanitized and reflective version that we often read about in "grief" books. She assured me that as much as I want to stab people who talk about "time healing" they are right. Time will heal. It will leave scars as a reminder, but the human body is designed to let go of the actual pain. If every time we thought about how much something hurt, emotional or physical, we felt the pain in the same way, we would all go crazy and implode. Sometimes that seems preferable. She told me that she can remember throwing herself down in the spot where her husband died and crying her guts out. She remembers that it was awful, but she can't "feel" it. This is why this needs to be written now, because I can feel it. I didn't write this book in any particular order. I started with what I thought would be the easy parts. Turned out, there are no easy parts. I've cried through every one of them. I'm crying now, although I'm trying not to because when I cry, I can't see what I am typing, and as much as my 8th grade typing teacher tried to drill into us that if you perfect your skills, you don't need to see what you are typing, I'm just not that good, or he lied.

I'm hoping that this book will give you a sense of what real, in your face, grief feels like. If you are grieving, I want you to know what may be in store and what the books don't tell you. If you are trying to help someone through their grief, I want you to give some thought before you do or don't do something.

Most of all, I want you to know that there is at least one person out there who gets it. The heart stopping, gut wrenching agony beyond anything you could ever imagine, the emptiness, the fear, the helplessness, wishing you could just disappear. I also want you to know that life goes on, the good and the bad; death changes everything and nothing. The you that you were before is dead and gone, but the new you is just beginning. I'd like to tell you to "embrace the suck" but that would really suck, so I won't bother. You do what's right for you and when the moment comes when you burst out laughing about something brought about by death, remember "I told you so."

The Real Face of Grief

Grief isn't beautiful. It isn't transcendent. It doesn't make you better than you were before. Grief doesn't make you kind or patient. There's no "Big grief for big love." Grief is ugly. It is raw. It is primeval.

Grief is rocking on the floor in the fetal position screaming "No! No!"

Grief is screaming into a pillow because you don't want the neighbors to call the cops.

Grief is sobbing hysterically until you begin to hyperventilate and can't open your eyes.

Grief is crying until you have no tears left.

Grief is wanting to throw something against the wall but stopping yourself because you know that if you start, you won't stop until there is nothing left to throw.

Grief is bursting into tears when you have your husband's car towed to the mechanic because, even though you know it's coming back, you see it as a hearse.

Grief is breaking down in tears because you just can't face doing one more thing alone.

Grief is for the first time since your husband's death and without thinking, sitting down at the dinner table, in his chair, and turning on the television. A trifecta of bad decisions resulting in hysterics just as you've taken a bite of mashed potatoes; tears running down your face and potatoes oozing out of your mouth. Then you realize that you look like something out of a bad Rom-Com and start to laugh. Laughing and crying and hoping (or not) that you don't choke to death.

Grief is opening the linen closet and seeing the blankets you carried back and forth to the hospital because the room was always cold, and you spend the day crying because you can't stop thinking about your husband being cold and alone.

Grief laughs at you. Grief rips out your heart, your liver, your kidneys, your intestines. It throws them to the ground, stomps on them, and with a vicious grin, shoves them back in and says "That was fun! Let's do it again!" Wham! You're back on your knees begging for it to stop.

Grief is solitary. Unlike in a break-up or divorce, there is no exchange. There is no comfort or satisfaction in thinking that the other person, who is still alive, is suffering in some way as well. In death, it's just you. No one else is crying or missing you. No one is angry at you. No one wishes they could die to be with you. Knowing that your husband is in heaven or some sort of afterlife or even just gone; that he is no longer in pain only increases the helplessness. You're crying and broken and, to put it bluntly, there's not a damn thing anyone can do about it.

Grief, even more so than the Law, is a jealous mistress. It will try to consume you, to destroy you. It is not a process or a journey to some sort of recovery. You may not realize it yet, but to enter into grief is to enter into war. Choose your battles wisely so that when the war is over, you will be the one standing with your sword plunged directly into the heart of grief.

Dead is Dead

Why do we use soft words? Is it to make the person grieving feel better? Or is it to make everyone else feel better, to distance them from reality?

She "lost" her husband. I didn't lose him. I know exactly where he is. Well, in reality, I know where about a tablespoon of him is. He's in a small can in a ceramic jar on my writing desk. The rest of him is supposedly somewhere in the ocean, but, as far as I know, he may have gone out with the trash. In any event, I'm not looking for him. I won't find him. He's not lost. He's dead.

He "passed away." First of all, "away" is superfluous because the definition of "pass" as a verb is to "go away," also "to die." I guess the idea being that when you die, you go away, far away, as in never coming back. Maybe it's because you're lost and can't find your way back? Regardless, call it what it is. He died. He's dead.

My "late" husband. He's not late (although he often was), he's dead, but I guess saying my "dead" husband makes people uncomfortable. Whatever. Making people feel comfortable about the death of my husband just isn't a priority.

Then there's my personal favorite, "transitioning." Transitioning is the word used when what is really being said is "He's dying. Get your ass over here!" Of course, they neglect to tell you that this whole "transitioning" thing may take hours, if not days, but better early than late (pun intended). I also wondered, and still do, into what, exactly, was he transitioning? Because Dean was a horror movie fan, the first thing that came to mind was that he was turning into a werewolf, in which case, he would have thought that totally cool. Of course, he didn't transition into a werewolf (at least not while I was there), but as far as I could tell, he didn't transition into anything else either. Although, lying on the bed with the sheet around him, if you gave him a crown and a sword, he did resemble King Arthur. Go figure.

Speaking of which, having nothing to do with soft words, once Dean died, he looked like himself again. His skin was smooth. His body had absorbed all the swelling. Except for the slightly blue lips and, well, being dead, he looked normal. It was both comforting and unsettling at the same time. I've since heard that this change is not unusual, but it was a surprise to me. I've never liked surprises.

I realize that was a bit of a digression, but the point is we shouldn't be afraid to call death what it is, namely, death. In fact, I'm going to digress further and tell you about talking with my neighbor who simply said, with calm acceptance, "We all die." He's right. Everyone who has lived has died. Everyone who is living, will die. Or as a friend, whose wife had died, said "No one gets out of here alive." I still think the werewolf thing would be cool.

What's God Got to Do With It?

I was raised Catholic, but the church and I parted ways a long time ago. I have no interest in any organized religion, and continue to be conflicted as to whether there is some sort of deity or creator or life force.

People have in turn said to me "God has a plan," "God needed Dean," "God knows what He is doing." These statements did not comfort me, they just pissed me off.

To say God has a plan, unless it is a generic plan such as "Live a good life" "Live up to your potential" "Be aware and open to opportunity," then, by definition, we no longer have free choice and God is making all the moves. If that is the case, then, as part of some sick plan, God at worst, murdered my husband or at best, allowed him to die. The same goes with God "needing" Dean. To do what? Prepare the Four Horsemen and their steeds for the Apocalypse? Besides, what kind of a God "needs" anything? Last I checked, "heaven" is a place where all needs are met. As to being told that God knows what he is doing, my response to that was "God doesn't know shit!" It was a short conversation.

Now, has Dean's death changed me and forced me to grow in ways I never wanted or expected? Of course. I will never be the person I was when Dean was alive because that person died right along with him. Would I trade any growth, future success, happiness etc. to have him back? Absolutely. But is that God's work? I don't think so. If you are a person of faith and that gets you through, then hold on to it. Just don't let other people tell you what you should believe and to whom you should pray. Even in the depths of my despair, my worst moments, I haven't prayed to God. The person I still call on is Dean. He is the one I ask to help me get through this. He is the one I tell how much I hurt, how much I miss him. I tell him that I can't do this, and I hear him telling me "Yes you can! Get your ass back in there and fight!" Even in death, he is still my cutman.

Don’t Tell Me What to Do

Sorry, but unless you've had a husband, wife, or life partner die, you don't get to have a voice. This is not to take away the pain of other devastating deaths, all are different. Strangely enough, those who have experienced the death of a spouse or life partner are the ones least likely to voice an opinion or give advice. This is probably because they remember wanting to punch people in the mouth when they tried to tell them "How it should be."

So, just don't:
Tell me how to grieve
Tell me how loooong it's going to take
Tell me what worked for you
Tell me I'm doing it wrong (usually in the form of "don't deny your feelings")
Tell me I have to have a memorial (so "we" can get closure)
Tell me I need to get rid of stuff
Tell me I shouldn't get rid of stuff
Tell me not to make any big decisions for at least a year, although, that one does sort of make sense, assuming we agree on what "big" means. But yes, if you see me selling off all my worldly possessions to live in a yurt, by all means, go ahead and speak up.

Bottom line, unless I ask for it, I don't need or want your advice, opinions, suggestions. What I do want is for you to just shut up, and if I need to talk, listen.

Piling On

Grief and grieving sucks. It sucks every day. Some days it sucks worse than others. What I don't need is a bunch of people, either in person or in writing, telling me how much more it is going to suck. It's like kicking a person when they are down. You know, every holiday, birthday, anniversary, is going to SUCK! In fact, every single day is going to present a new first and that is going to SUCK! Every time you open a closet, cupboard, drawer, something will remind you of Dean. In reality, every time I open a closet, cupboard, drawer, I am more likely to say, "So, that's where he put that." Then there's the coup de gras, the kick to the head. THE SECOND YEAR WILL BE WORSE! The first year you are in a daze; it's not until the second year that it really hits you. What the fuck? Like I need to hear that or any of this. I am not stupid. I have the sense to know that days that were special to us may be a little tougher to get through than say, Tuesday (although Tuesdays have sucked too). But beating me over the head with how HARD it is going to be only makes it a certainty and fills me with dread. I might as well just crawl in a hole now and get it over with. The truth is that no one knows how it is really going to be. Maybe if I go into it with a positive, but cautious attitude, it won't cripple me. Maybe just leave my options open and take the days as they come. Because I have heard it so much, the apprehension is already there.

Halloween, which was (and probably still is) Dean's favorite holiday is coming up. I won't decorate like he did (I never really liked Halloween, but indulged him, because that is what you do for people you love) but our wreath is on the door. We never get trick or treaters, so that's not an issue.

If I get bummed and cry, so be it, hell, I'm crying now. But maybe, I'll put on some spooky music, raise a glass and remember how much fun he would have. I won't know until I get there, but I do know that dreading it will only make misery certain. *

Next is Thanksgiving. We hosted it for over 30 years. Well, no more. We always talked about how much we would like to have it just be us. No family, just us. Well, that's not going to happen or rather, it will be just us, but in different planes. So, I'm going out with friends. If it gets too hard, I'll leave, but right now, I plan to have a good time and be thankful for what I have and for what Dean and I shared. Many people aren't that fortunate. **

As far as Christmas is concerned, I just know it's going to be a lot cheaper. ***

*It was fine. I had track practice. It was a little sad, but nothing horrible.

** Also fine. In fact, the group was so eclectic that I couldn't help but think "and I thought I was strange." I suspect Dean was laughing his ass off.

***Because I skipped Christmas, it was just a Monday. I had track practice, a friend came by, and I worked in the yard. No family to entertain, no food to cook. It was one of the most pleasant days in a long time.

Comforting Others

Let me make something clear, it was my husband who died, so you need to get over it.

Dean knew a lot, and I mean a lot, of people. He had circles of friends from various times and places in his life. He was, and still is, a legend (for better or worse) in all of them. Fortunately, I was able to create phone / text trees for most of the groups. But there were a few where I just had to break the news myself. Not as easy as it sounds. Dean didn't keep contacts in his phone. He memorized the numbers! (And you thought I was kidding about being a legend.) So, for some of his friends, I had to wait until they called or texted his phone. That bandaged wound that was starting to scab? Time to rip it off and start the bleeding all over again. The calls all started the same with me saying "This is Jeanne, Dean's wife" and bursting into tears while the person on the other end keeps saying "Oh my God, what's wrong?" and me finally getting out "Dean. Dean. He died." "What? What? How? When?" And then I would manage to get out the story, both of us in tears, but eventually ending in a nice conversation.

One call, however, did not go that well. The person on the other end started screaming "No! No! You're lying to me! You don't understand! He saved my life! Without Dean, I would have died!" And in the background, things crashing to the floor and breaking. I found myself in the position of trying to comfort this person and talk them off the ledge. Once we hung up, I spent the night worrying that something really bad would happen. Fortunately, I got a text in the morning apologizing, which of course put me back in the role of comforter.

I can't blame the people getting the news, and I can't tell you that if you are one of those people, keep your cool. I just want you to know that if you are the one making the call, be prepared, you may have to step out of your grief and comfort someone else.

My Husband Was Not a Cat

I received a sympathy card, a nice thing, that included a full-page type written letter about the death of a cat. Seriously.

Now, Dean and I were, and I'm assuming he still is, as am I, animal lovers. In fact, as a general rule, I like animals more than people. Dean was a little more forgiving with the human race. Anyway, in our 30+ years together, we shepherded several dogs and several horses into the great beyond. I cried every time. Dean could be with them, often laying down beside them, holding their heads and / or paws. That was beyond me. I made up for it when Dean died, and looking forward, if I ever have to see a pet into the great beyond, I will do so with grace and dignity. But, please be advised, in no place and at no time will the death of a pet, or of a hundred pets, equal the death of a husband. I am quite sure that they felt they were somehow trying to provide comfort and understanding, but what I really think is that they were using my grief to provide them a cathartic opportunity. At the time, however, I was speechless. Obviously, I've gotten past that, and actually find it a little sad. The message, however, is do not compare your grief to mine. It's been said that the worst grief is your own. I think that is true. I have also noticed that the only people who make comparisons or give you advice are those who have not been where you are. The people who have been where you are know to just shut the fuck up. So, if you haven't been there, see the previous sentence.

Comparing Grief

This is a weird one and you are only allowed to do it with a trusted friend who has been where you are. I don't know why we feel compelled to make these comparisons. I am sure there is some psychological reason for it, but understanding it doesn't change the fact that we want to do it. Maybe it is as simple as trying to make ourselves feel better. In any event, my conversation was with a friend who, although her husband was very ill, did not expect to come home and find him dead. We decided that having your, apparently healthy, husband drop dead while you were out of town was really bad. Having your husband killed in an accident where the damage was such that you couldn't see him was worse. We were a little conflicted about having your husband die after a long illness versus only knowing for a couple of days. We couldn't decide if being able to prepare was better than living with hope that would be dashed to the ground. Ugly choice. Dying at home or elsewhere? Does it matter how long you were married? Does it matter how old you are? What if you are very old and maybe only have a few years left versus very young with many years left. We couldn't come to a conclusion on any of that. What we did decide is being able to say good bye was a gift to be treasured. It doesn't make it easier, there is no "closure", maybe it's just a little more complete. Hopefully, I will one day think about that moment, looking into his eyes, telling him I love him, and that he could go and that I would be okay, without dissolving into tears. I don't know when that will be, but it's not yet. It all sucks.

Grading on a Curve

Don't be surprised when friends, and others, usually behind your back, grade your progress. "She's doing so well." "And it's only been 7 months." "Can you believe he's even thinking about dating?" "She really seems to be stuck." "He doesn't look so good."

In my case, it revolved mostly around the fact that I was on the track the next night and in competition the next week. "I can't believe you are competing so soon." "I couldn't do that." "Good for you." No one truly understood that it was something that I **had** to do. That every track practice started with me in tears and every night in my hotel room the same.

I'm not sure the psychology behind the need to monitor others' grief. I do think that when people tell you "You're doing so well," they are, in their way, trying to encourage and support you as well as giving themselves permission to not worry about you. No one is going to come up to you and say "Gee, you look like shit. Not moving forward much are you?" They'll say that amongst themselves, behind your back. If it helps to have people tell you that you are doing well, then embrace it. Otherwise, ignore them. They only see the curated you. They don't know what the hell they're talking about.

Death: A Five-Star Review

Death is a money maker, and in today's world, any money maker is going to want 5 stars.

"Would you be willing to share your experience and leave a review on Google? It only takes 30 seconds. Here is the Link." That is a direct quote from a text message from the people who handled Dean's cremation. It was couched in terms of helping more families like mine. I can tell you how to help more families like mine. Don't ask me to give you a review on Google! And certainly not just three freaking months after my husband died. What the hell?

Now, if someone asked me about my experience (with the cremation part, not the Dean dying part), I would say that it was generally a good, albeit strange, one. Dean and I made our arrangements several years ago (and no, didn't plan on needing them quite this soon), after a neighbor's daughter died unexpectedly. They were at a complete loss, and Dean helped them through. I'm glad we did because it was one less thing I had to deal with.

The men who picked up Dean's body were kind and considerate. I'm sure they see every kind of reaction, so they went with the flow of our jovial reception. *

*Yes, jovial. When Dean died, it was standing room only. Most had been there all day. Dean wasn't responsive but there was crying, laughing, and story telling along with giving Dean rations of shit for, well, just because.

What I didn't know was that I would have to go to the company's office, do more paperwork, and make decisions about things like how many death certificates I wanted. They gave me one for free (read included in the price, so not really free) and I, on the advice of a friend, ordered seven more. I still have six.

The week after Dean died, I was asked to come to the office to finalize paperwork. Going to the "showroom," as that's the only way I can describe it, was an experience unto itself. It was really quiet. I mean really quiet. Dim lighting and soft music. I thought I might have stumbled into somebody's funeral. I was seated in a side room and given a bottle of water and a box of Kleenex. I sort of got it, but huh? I'd rather have had a Hershey Bar. Without almonds. Having no idea what was going to happen, I just sat there looking around the room where artfully displayed were the various urns in which, for a fee, many for a big fee, your loved one could be housed for all eternity. Did you know there's a thing where you can grow a tree in your loved one's ashes? I did not know that. I wish I did not know that. There was also a lovely jewelry display. At least I thought it was lovely until I realized that all of the items were designed to hold your loved one's ashes. I know and respect that some people might find that comforting, but it just creeped me out. Eventually we got down to business. Complete with PowerPoint. Yes, that's right. PowerPoint presentation of decisions to be made and documents to be signed. Hysterical, as in you have got to be kidding, laughter was bubbling, but I tamped it down, and held on to a straight face. Did I still want Dean scattered at sea? Yes. Did I want to go on the boat (for an extra fee)? No. Did I want to make an event of it and bring a group (for an extra, extra fee)? No. I did ask that a very small portion of his ashes be kept for me to scatter at a place and time of my choosing. I explained to the kind man that Dean would have preferred a Viking Funeral complete with flaming boat, but that since we couldn't pull that off, cremation was the next best thing. He either didn't get the joke or just thought I was crazy, maybe both. Needless to say, I signed on the dotted line and got the hell out of there. Even though the experience was positive, sort of, I guess, I'm still not doing a review on Google. One has to draw the line somewhere.

You Don't Know Me

I've gone back and forth about including this as it seems kind of strange as well as unique. But, after much thought, although it still seems strange, it probably isn't unique and you may very well experience it. So here goes.

Apparently Dean talked about me a lot. I've heard over and over "Dean talked about you all the time." He talked about my work, my hobbies, the races I ran, and who knows what else.

Many people said "I feel like I know you," but some actually said "We have so much in common. We should get together." Uh, no.

What they don't understand is that what they heard was a curated version. They didn't hear about my quirks (although if they had, it might have solved the "Let's hang out" problem), my fears, hopes and dreams. I also understand that some people are trying to hold on to Dean and I am the only connection, but again, no.

Fortunately, no one who doesn't actually know me followed through, so I don't feel bad about not responding. However, in an opposite vein to wanting to hold on to Dean through me, some avoid me completely. There are people who always said "Hi" to me, who now walk past me as though I don't exist. I don't know if they were just nice to me before because they wanted to stay in Dean's good graces, or maybe, by not acknowledging me, they can pretend he is still alive but on a long vacation? I have no idea. I just know it happens.

Memorialize This!

Dean hated memorials. He understood why people wanted to have them, but he hated them. He hated the photos on a continuous loop, the tributes, the speeches. He hated how everyone in death becomes a saint. He just wanted someone to say "He was a real asshole." or "She gave new meaning to the word 'bitch'." His favorite obituary was one that said "He slipped off the raft." He often told friends, "Just put me out with the garbage."

In any event, everyone wants to know when you are having the memorial. Every card, every text. "Is there a memorial?" "Please include me." My token text said "No memorial pending," but that didn't stop anybody. They would respond, "Well when you do …."

One person offered to host the memorial, as in the space would hold 350 people and I was welcome to have it there. Of course, I would still be the one organizing the event, inviting the guests, and footing the bill, but hey, at least I would have a venue. Even better was "You don't have to do it now. You can do it a year from now." Really? Like I want to dredge up all this shit a year from now. I don't think so. Then the capper. The memorial isn't really for Dean, it's for us. Every fiber of my being wanted to scream "Then have your fucking memorial. I don't care. I won't be offended. I even have a venue. If you need a memorial for your closure, then have at it. Just leave me the fuck alone!" This same person came at me again 6 months later. "I'd like to have a conversation about having an informal memorial for Dean." I'm sorry, YOU want to have a conversation with ME about my dead husband? What part of "NO" didn't you understand? My response was a polite version of "Have one! Just leave me alone." I chose not to point out that I am moving forward, not backward. The point is that people won't respect your feelings, or they will decide that you really didn't know what you were saying because of your "grief" and once you come to your senses ... Fuck them!

Now, I did have a very small get together (I call it his "Going away" party) of Dean's closest friends. Mostly the guys. Guys with whom he walked through the fire, the guys who stepped out on the mat. (Dean taught San Soo, hand to hand combat, for many years. Many of the guys had been with him all those many years.) It was a Viking funeral, complete with paper ship with a bit of Dean's ashes which I set on fire so the Valkyries could usher Dean to Valhalla.

Dean wasn't Norse, so this bears some explaining. First and foremost, Dean was a Scotsman. He always said he was born about seven hundred years too late. He always wanted to go to Blair Castle, the ancestral home of his Clan, and say "I'm back! Get the hell out!" I considered a Scottish funeral, but a Scottish funeral involves bagpipes and as much as I love a good bagpipe, it's just too damn sad, so no to that. Next, Dean was German, but unless there is a lot of beer and polka music, the Germans are a pretty taciturn bunch. So, again, no. Next, Dean was a Jersey boy, and even though I have enough baseball bats for all, I didn't think the local citizenry would appreciate a rumble in my backyard. So, once more, no. Lastly, although Dean had a soft heart and collected damaged souls, both human and animal, and did what he could to heal them, he was, when necessary, a badass. He was fearless and uncompromising in his belief of what is right and good. Those who were his friends were protected. I know without doubt, he would have died for me, he would have killed for me, without hesitation. He also loved boats. So, the Vikings. It was the perfect sendoff. Dean would have enjoyed it. Maybe he did.

The Things People Say

No one has any idea what to say, when they learn your spouse has died. The "go to" is "I'm sorry for your loss." It's no one's fault, but it is so inadequate, so soft. Because it was mostly people with whom I am not close who said it, I responded with a token "Thank you." Occasionally, I would add "It really sucks."

For some people who know where I live, the next question would be "What are you going to do with the house? I mean, it's a big house for one person." Huh? Are you serious? First, it's my home and I am going to live there. Second, how is it any of your business? You looking to buy?

Along with having those having no tact, are the "questioners." I ran into a couple at the grocery store who had heard about Dean's death through the grapevine. The wife said all the "appropriate" things, but the husband started peppering me with questions. "When did he die?" "How old was he?" "What did he die of?" "What did his doctors say?" I think I stood there (remember, I'm at the freaking grocery store) babbling something while trying not to cry until his wife said "It's too soon." Ya think? And, again, how is that any of your business?

Then there are the "blamers." They think they know what happened and believe they have the right to voice their opinion. One of these had the nerve to flag me down, as I was driving away from my house. She started with the "appropriate" things but then went on to tell me that Dean should have been more open about his illness because he denied people the opportunity to say "good-bye." What the fuck? Who do you think you are criticizing my dead husband about something you know nothing about? It was a good thing she wasn't standing in front of my car because I simply said I had to go and floored it.

For some, it's not so much a question of tact, but a complete inability to see the effect their words are having on you. Most of the people at the gym (a very small gym where everyone knew / knows Dean and me) were very respectful. They left me alone or only said a quick word. My trainer did his best to protect me and stop people from approaching, but some people were determined to have their say. One woman accosted (that's the only word that describes it) me saying the usual plus "great guy" blah blah. I managed to extricate myself and went back to my workout. A bit later, she came at me again asking "How long were you married?" The tears started. She patted my shoulder and said "Well, you're still married in your heart." Really? Tell that to the IRS!

The strangest one (I don't even remember who said it) was "Well, if one of you had to die, it's a good thing it was Dean, because if it was you, he wouldn't have been able to handle it." It didn't register at the time (I think it was actually while Dean was dying, oops, transitioning), but later I wondered what the hell did that mean? That Dean was weak? That he loved me more? I think it was meant to be some sort of a compliment but I honestly have no idea. One thing I do know, don't say shit like that.

Hoping to Die

Every night I say the same thing. I tell the universe that if it wants to take me, go ahead, please. I then tell Dean that I don't think the universe is going to cooperate, so please watch over me. I then tell him that I love him and that I miss him.

I've never really feared death. I figured that when I died, I'd either go to some afterlife or just cease to be. The fear has always been the idea of suffering. I'm still not a fan of suffering, but any residual fear of death I might have had has been eliminated.

I don't want to die in that I would commit suicide. That has never crossed my mind and frankly would take more energy that I can muster. * It's more of just not wanting to be here. A friend, who has been in my place, told me about walking across a bridge and stopping to look down. As she looked at the water, she wondered what the chances were, if she just fell off, of dying. She figured not much, as the bridge was too close to the water. She just kept walking.

One night I was lying in bed and heard the police helicopter flying overhead. I remember wondering if someone was going to break into the house and kill me. I wasn't scared. I didn't really think it would happen, but I was ok with it.

These are the kind of random thoughts that wander through my mind. How can I just not be here anymore?

On the other hand, waking up has moved from despair to somewhere between disappointment and apathy. I guess that's progress. Every morning, I wake up and just want to go back to sleep, preferably the "big sleep." I don't want to face the day. I have yet (notice the use of the word "yet") to look forward to anything. I say good morning to Dean. I go through my routine, alone. I shower, dress, and look at my list for the day, alone. I do what needs to be done. I go the gym. I go to the track. I eat dinner, alone. I go to bed alone. I say the same prayer and wake up disappointed, alone.

***Please, if you are severely depressed and / or suicidal, seek help! Call or text 988 in the United States (Every country has an equivalent) for the Suicide and Crisis Lifeline to speak to a mental health professional.**

Counseling Myself

Some have suggested that I consider grief counseling or some sort of support group. I don't think it's because they think I "need" it, but because it seems to be the thing to suggest. If it's something that helps you, go for it. In any event, not my thing. I don't know what talking to someone for an hour a week would do for me that I can't do for myself. My grieving doesn't confine itself to a time and place, plus, if I'm not feeling sad or thinking about Dean, I don't want to have to deal with it just because it's "my time." I also know what would be said, encouraged, discouraged, whatever. So, I just play both roles as needed. It's kind of weird to be counseling yourself during a crying jag or fit of anger, but it works for me. Sometimes, I even make sense.

Metaphorically Speaking

Everyone, myself included, wants to have some way to describe grief and grieving. The two most popular are "journey" and "process." I despise those words. I despised them before Dean died and nothing has changed. I'm a destination, results, kind of person. I'm all for training, studying, practicing etc., but as a means to an end. Just get me there. One of my sayings is "The only people who are interested in the journey are those who don't know where they are going." But even if you embrace the journey not destination concept, grief isn't a journey and no one wants to embrace it. Grief is a living hell and the only thing you want to do is get it over with. Of course, that brings in the guilt of "does that mean I didn't love him enough?" If my love was heroic, then my grief must be heroic (yes there are books on that). If I don't grieve properly, I won't be evolved, transcendent, or more beautiful than before (yes, there are books on that too).

My initial response to "How are you doing?" was "OK" or "Hanging in there." Then I started thinking that maybe I needed to be more positive, so I switched to "I'm healing." I thought the change in perspective might help. I think the only people it helped were the recipients because they could comfort themselves with "Oh good. She's doing better." It didn't do shit for me. I then tried thinking that wounds will heal, but will leave a scar (less guilt about not loving enough). I think the concept is a pretty good one, and very Zen, but in reality, not helpful.

Then there's the hamster wheel. Millions of people in this world are going through this at the same time, but we are all on our own wheels. We just run and run and run until we are so tired that we just start spinning in circles. Spin,

spin, spin until we can't even hold on anymore and fly off the wheel and land in a tangled heap on the ground. We just lie there thinking, "I just can't do this anymore" until we are forced to crawl back on the wheel and start the whole thing over again.

I also went through the "ultramarathon" phase where I likened grief to a race that has no defined end. You didn't sign up for it, didn't train for it, but all of a sudden, you're in it. You don't have the proper clothing or shoes. It's called a race, but there is no competition. You're alone. There is no finish line in sight. All you are told is that you will know it when you get there. There is no time out for weather. The course is not marked. Parts are flat and dry, others are wet, muddy, and straight uphill. There are boulders and pits. You can't see beyond your own feet, so you have no idea what is coming. You only find out when you are in it, often flat on your face, bloody and broken, asking "Why me?" The only saving grace is that, if you are lucky, there are aid stations. These are your friends. They can support you, but they can't do it for you, and, as I learned, they're not always there. What became readily apparent is that people have lives. Just because yours stopped, detoured, went right off a cliff, theirs did not. So, they won't always be there when you think they will. There will be times, many of them, when you will be alone, tired, hungry, thirsty, and even if you cry out "Please help me!" no one will answer.

The turning point for me came after having been tackled and side swiped by grief one too many times. I started crying one afternoon and cried into the evening. The next morning, I started crying again. Then I got a text that said, in part, "You seem to be holding up." HA! If you could see me now! There I was, a miserable sobbing pile of grief who suddenly decided, instead of surrendering to what I now perceived as the enemy, “This means war!”

I started screaming at Dean that I hate that he doesn’t miss me. I hate that he isn’t sad, not for himself or for me. That it isn’t fair that he’s wherever, and I’m stuck here in this hellhole. (Not really fair to him, but I was really pissed.) Then, I turned on Grief, screaming “Who the fuck do you think you are?” “I will not do this!” Grief responded that I would do this, because it is the process, it is the journey. I responded “Fuck you! And your process, and your journey, and the horse you road in on!” “This is my day off, and you will not take it from me!” Grief, with all the menace it could muster, said “Oh you think so? My job is to tear you apart and leave you bleeding. It’s the only way you will heal.” Not willing to let Grief have the last word, and with as much menace as I could muster shot back, “Well, I’ve got two words for you ‘Shut the fuck up!’”

Even during the interchange, I wondered if I was losing my mind by having an argument with Grief and playing both parts. I’m sure some therapist would drone on about “normal” and “process” or try to sedate me, but I’m pretty sure I could hear Dean in the background yelling “That’s what I’m talking about! That’s my girl!” Needless to say, I’ve felt better ever since, and Grief has been walking on eggshells.

It's 2:00 a.m.
Do You Know Where Your Friends Are?

“Whatever you need.” “24/7” “Just give me a call.” “Anything I can do.”

I can’t tell you how many times someone said one of those phrases or something like it. Do yourself a favor, and take it with a grain of salt. Most people, at the time, think they mean it. Most people are assuming you will never take them up on it. It’s kind of a reflex thing to say. Fortunately, I have some very good friends and friends who took their promise to Dean to take care of me very seriously. I was confident that if I put out a 2:00 a.m. distress call, they would all come running. But, for the day in, day out battles, my comrades in arms were not the people I thought they would be.

If you had asked me a few years ago to list the people that would stand by me through thick and thin, never miss a beat and be rocks during a storm, it would have been an easy list to make. It also would have been completely wrong. For the people you see every day, it’s easier for them. Seeing you is the reminder to ask how you are doing or to send the “Thinking of you” text. For the people that you don’t see every day, no matter how close you think you are, you are not front and center in their lives.

Initially, there were daily check-ins. Then they became weekly, and at just over three months, with a couple of exceptions, they pretty much stopped. Even at Thanksgiving and Christmas, only two people checked in with me. They were not people that would have been on my list. The holidays themselves weren’t that difficult, but being forgotten kind of stung.

I'm not sure why people forget about you, other than they have lives and out of sight out of mind. I don't think anyone means to be hurtful, I just don't think they think about it. It may be connected to whether you appear to be coping, and therefore, they don't need to worry about you, or if you're not coping, they shy away from the pain. I'd like to think that when my name popped up on people's phones, they didn't think "Oh, God, no," but maybe they did. I've avoided reaching out. I think there have only been two or three times when it got so bad that I called someone, when I physically could not stop crying. I remind myself that even though there are probably millions of people going through this, in my small world, there is only me. My friends have lives that don't include my daily trauma. Plus, there is nothing they can do. It can't be fixed. It is what it is.

They say it's in times of crisis that you really find out who your friends are. Many of both Dean's and my friends came through in different ways at different times, but there is only one who has been an absolute rock. She has never forgotten me, never failed me. She has come through like a champ, whether I needed it or not. She knows when to be quiet and when to say outrageous things to make me laugh. She sends silly texts with silly pictures. She brings me presents and gives me food, sometimes right out of her refrigerator. Japanese sweet potato anyone? She wouldn't have been on the list. She is now. At the top.

Wasn’t Expecting That

As I've mentioned, Dean didn't keep contacts in his phone. In addition to texts or calls from people I know, there were numerous texts and calls from people I did not know, including people who had heard about his death but did not believe it, so they were calling him to make sure that it was just a rumor. Those were a special kind of fun. I wasn't ready for that. I eventually had to set up an auto text to let people know that Dean had died and that no memorial was pending. Unfortunately, that always created the response text of "Oh no! I'm so sorry" and so on. I felt compelled to respond to those texts with at least a "Thank you." I left his phone on through the new year, figuring that if there were any people out there who hadn't found out, the holidays would be the time they would surface. Fortunately, no one did, so just after the new year, I shut down his phone. It was a bit sad, but more of a relief that I no longer had to dread looking at it and having to go through the pain of telling another person.

I never thought about how much we communicated. In the early days, we didn't have cell phones, so there wasn't the instant communication we have now. Less than a week after Dean died, I was on a plane to Pittsburgh to compete in the National Senior Games in the 200m sprint. Dean had made it clear that I was going to Pittsburgh "No matter what" so, even though crawling into a hole and dying felt preferable, I went. Some people have said that they would pick up their phone to call or text, forgetting for a moment that the person had died. I never experienced that. What did happen was I was bombarded with thoughts of "I'd be texting Dean to let him know I'm on the plane" "I'm at the hotel" and so on. The worst moment was when I arrived in Pittsburgh and was going down the escalator. As you go down, you pass a replica skeleton of a Tyrannosaurus Rex. Dean loved dinosaurs so that was something I would have taken a picture of and texted to him. Instead, I burst into tears. After that, it didn't become easier, I was just better prepared.

Fortunately, in Pittsburgh, I was with people who knew Dean and what had happened. So, I could talk about him and, if things got too intense and I walked away or whatever, they understood. Not so the next trip. About three months after Dean died, I went to London. This was a trip that was originally set for March 2020. It had been postponed six times and was finally going to happen. The trip didn't involve Dean (I probably wouldn't have been able to handle that), as it was a trip related to a hobby of mine. Only one person, the leader / organizer, knew Dean and what had happened. The other twelve women knew nothing. The stress of dodging, bobbing, weaving in and out of conversations that would lead to questions about "husband" was horrific. Too new, too raw. I could envision the conversations, "My husband and I went …" "Oh, what does your husband do?" "Uh, well, now, nothing. He's dead." Now, there's a conversation stopper. Having become used to giving in to my emotions as needed, not doing so was excruciating. I would get through the day and then go to my hotel room and just cry. I don't regret the trip. I just have to separate the trip from the emotional toll.

I've also mentioned about being forgotten. Like I said, it was surprising and kind of hurt, but it wasn't devastating. I guess I sort of expected it along with feeling the third wheel or the occasional pity invite. What I didn't expect was to be flat out excluded. The short version is that I was not invited to a friend's wedding. He was a friend of Dean's long before I met Dean. He was in our wedding. Dean was the person who came to the rescue when his wife died. He came to all our parties. He was at Dean's going away party. I gave him one of Dean's collections. I can't begin to understand the thought process of excluding me. I can't believe it was done with any sort of malice. I knew he was engaged. I'd met his fiancé. I knew other people who were invited so it's not like I wouldn't find out. It cut me like a knife. I must have cried for 2 days. Maybe he thought it would be too painful for me. Maybe, me, as a reminder of Dean, would be too painful for him. I wish he would have talked to me. I've thought about asking him, but to what end?

Amaryllis by Morning

I never know what will set me off. After Dean died, I went through his things like a whirling dervish. Clothes, shoes, no problem. Cub scout uniform that his mom had kept, no problem. Desk drawers full of notebooks, pens, ink, no problem. Passport from 1984, problem. Full on, down to the knees gut punch. I didn't even know him in 1984, but he looked so young, so happy, so full of life. I fell apart.

When Dean was in the hospital, because the room temperature was so unpredictable, I would bring him blankets from home. Bring them there, bring them home, wash and repeat. After he died, the blankets went back into the closet. I saw them, moved them dozens of times, nothing. Then about 5 months in, I opened the closet and seeing those blankets crippled me for 2 days! All I could think about is him being in the hospital and being cold. (Which he obviously wasn't because I made sure he had the blankets!)

Then came the amaryllis. For several years, at Christmas, our neighbor would bring us one of those wax encased amaryllis bulbs. You don't have to do anything for it, just set it in the sun. We always kept it in the kitchen. Much to his dismay, every time Dean came into the kitchen, I would start singing "Amaryllis by Morning" (apologies to George Strait and "Amarillo by Morning"). He would always laugh and say something like "That is so wrong." Later, he would give me grief because he couldn't get "That damn song" out of his head. When my neighbor gave me the amaryllis this year, it didn't hit me until I put it in its spot in the kitchen. All I could think of was "Amaryllis by Morning." It broke me, but I sang it anyway, just in case Dean was listening.

Medium Well

Anyone who knows me, and probably even those who don't, would never describe me as woo-woo. I've always been a grounded, practical person. When people would complain about smog, I would always say that smog was ok, because I didn't trust air that I couldn't see. (Yes, I know smog isn't air and no, I'm not a fan of smog, so environmentalists can stand down) Although I love horror stories, I never really bought into the supernatural and hauntings. Dean, on the other hand, was a huge fan of the TV series "Ancient Aliens." He had all the episodes on DVD. I think part of the reason he watched them was just to see me roll my eyes. In any event, two books got me thinking, *Big Magic* by Elizabeth Gilbert and *From the Corner of His Eye* by Dean Koontz. *Big Magic* got me thinking about ideas and how they come to one person or another; if you don't grab the idea when it passes by, someone else will. More of a universal force kind of thing. *From the Corner of His Eye* made me think about quantum mechanics, which, according to Richard Feynman, no one understands anyhow. Truer words. What I like and want to believe is that there are parallel universes where, as Barty, the protagonist in *From the Corner of His Eye*, says we are living lives in many places; there may be a place where Dean didn't die and our lives continue. Of course, by the same token, there may be a place where I died and he has to go on. I don't think there is a perfect answer. What I do know is that the evening after Dean died, he sent me a sign. The fact that it involved a spoon and a cup still puzzles me, but there it is. Without going into kitchen schematics, suffice to say, it was physically impossible for the spoon and cup to have done what they did. The spoon landed on the kitchen floor and the cup was balanced on another cup that was hanging on a hook on the wall. In hindsight, I should have photographed it, but I was too stunned. I simply looked to the ceiling (because we all look up to talk to dead people) and said “Really? You threw a spoon at me?” The spoon and cup now sit on my writing desk.

After telling the spoon story to a friend of mine who admittedly ranks high on the woo-woo scale, she, figuring my mind had expanded, bought me a session with a medium. He had been recommended to her, and she felt it helped her with some unresolved issues involving the death of a family member. Desperate times and all that, I made an appointment. The session was over the phone, and the only thing the medium knew was my name. Googling my name alone, won’t get you far, and certainly won’t get you anything about Dean. Admittedly, I wanted to believe. I wanted to connect with Dean. I also heard the voice inside my head saying this is the most ridiculous thing I’ve ever done. The medium asked me no questions. He told me the only response required was “That makes sense” or “That doesn’t make sense.” There was no TV drama of “I’m sensing there is a Robert, Rick, a name with a R in the room.” He suggested that I write everything down. Again, without excruciating detail because it would take too long and isn’t the point, just about everything, right down to the dog with Dean, made sense. Could it all have been lucky guesses? I suppose. But eventually, the luck must run out. Even going through my notes months later and looking with a critical eye, things still hold. There was one pretty big thing, however, that made no sense at all. The medium told me that sometimes a spirit (for lack of a better term), will reach out to someone who is in the social circle of the person to whom they are connected, and to keep that in mind, if things didn’t make sense. I thought and thought about the information and got nothing, no connection anywhere, until about a month later when everything fell into place. I was having dinner with friends and one started talking about a friend of his that he wished Dean could have met. As he told me the story, I felt chills, goosebumps, the whole deal. I said to my friend, "I think Dean has met him. When did this happen?" It was 10 days before my session that his friend had died exactly as described by the medium. The experience did not eliminate my grief, but it did provide food for thought. It also nudged me over on the woo-woo scale. Now do I think there are people out there scamming and taking advantage of people at their most vulnerable times? Absolutely. On the other hand, I think Shakespeare got it right when Hamlet said "There are more things in Heaven and Earth, Horatio, than are dreamt of in your philosophy." As with many things, I am now open to possibility.

One Track Mind - Part I

Some of you may know me from my book *Spike Up! Becoming an Athlete at 60.* For those of you who don't, I have one word, Amazon. In any case, I am a weight lifter, sprinter, and obstacle course racer. A friend, who had just read the book, asked if I thought my continued athleticism had anything to do with how I was handling Dean's death. Having had her husband die a few years earlier, she thought that I, at 3 months out, seemed more in control and "further along" than she was at the same time. I said that I really hadn't thought about it and really had no basis of comparison. It's not like I had a husband die when exercise wasn't a part of my life.

Having given it some thought since then, I think the answer is yes and no. Thanks a lot, right? No, in the sense that I don't think exercise is moving me along the grief trail any more quickly. I think that's going to be what it's going to be. But yes, in that it helps to keep me sane and puts me in regular contact with supportive friends. During Dean's illness, with little exception, I never stopped my routine. Just before Dean went into the hospital, I competed in the Pasadena Senior Games earning gold medals in the 100m and 200m. A few days after he was admitted, I competed in the Pasadena Senior Games power lifting and bench pressed my way to a gold medal. Every day, I would go to the hospital, then to the gym or track, then back to the hospital. Keep in mind, this was while I had hope and didn't know that the worst thing I couldn't imagine was coming straight at me. Also, during this time, the issue of Pittsburgh kept rearing its ugly head. I had qualified the year before to compete at the National Senior Games. Whenever the subject would come up, Dean would say "You're going to Pittsburgh." As the days passed, I kept shortening the trip, finally to the point where I would go, run one race, and come home. The guys had worked it out so that someone would be with him at all times. Needless to say, none of it mattered in the end. Now, I kind of wonder whether he let go when he did to make damn sure I went.

Dean died Wednesday afternoon. Knowing what he expected of me and fearing what would happen if I didn't fulfill his wish, I was on the track Thursday, Friday, and Sunday, each time in tears. Monday, I was on a plane to Pittsburgh. It's pretty much a blur, but I ran. I ran the preliminaries, set a new PR (personal record) and qualified for the finals. I ran the finals and came home with a 7th place finish in my first national competition. I'm pretty sure he was proud of me.

The next thing I had to gear up for was San Diego which was 2 months away. I hadn't been to the gym since all hell broke loose. Going back was tough. Dean was a presence at the gym. He had an office where he saw clients. He knew just about everyone. From what I heard, within 30 minutes of his death, the entire gym knew. My first day back, I went in, walked over to my trainer and started to cry. I said "I don't know if I can do this." Then, I took a deep breath and decided, yes I can and yes I will. Most people were very respectful and gave me my space. My trainer made sure to head people off and protect me. I muddled through, sometimes with a smile, other times with tears running down my face and still other times with tears running down both our faces. It was easier on the track. Only coach knew the situation. I wasn't on a team. I'd show up, often in tears. We'd cry together and then get to work. The focus necessary kept me from thinking about anything else. I always felt better afterwards.

We went to San Diego and I had the race of my life. I cried a little on the way there and then also on the way back because, if Dean had been alive, he would have had a victory present and special meal ready. He always believed more in me, and I'm sure still does, than I do in myself. In between, however, I was so focused on what I was there to do, I didn't think about him at all, and when I crossed the finish line in the 200m, I felt more alive than I had since the troubles began. That feeling has faded, but at least I know it is possible.

So back to the original question. I think it is a combination of things. Being physical definitely makes me feel better. I feel less restless and more accomplished, but I don't know whether, if I was doing it alone, it would have the same effect. I think being with friends gives it the extra boost with the end result being both physical and emotional redirection. It may not make the trip faster, but it does make it a little bit, in little parts easier. I'll take it.

One Track Mind - Part II

Part I was written about 4 months after Dean died. I left it as it was written because I don't want to be guilty of what I think most grief books are, that is writing from the long view, with a long view perspective. However, just before Christmas, about 2 weeks before what I thought of as "half-way", something changed. I started to feel more like myself. I stopped crying every day. It wasn't a gradual change but as though some sort of switch had been flipped. While out with a friend, I told her what had happened and she commented "Your brain is rewiring." I recalled that I had told her about the book *The Grieving Brain* by Mary-Frances O'Connor. * It was the only book that I had read that was of any use to me, because it gave a scientific explanation for what I was experiencing. The neuroscience of the brain is obviously complex, but the takeaway from the book was, for me, simple. As infants, our brain thinks that when we can't see mom, she is gone. This causes us distress, often in the form of crying, until mom returns. Eventually, our brain begins to understand that, even though we can't see mom, she isn't gone, she's coming back. With the death of a loved one, it's as though the brain has to work in reverse and rewire to understand that, in this case, the person isn't coming back. Even if at a conscious level, I know / knew Dean is / was dead and not coming back, my subconscious didn't. Every time there was a clash, so to speak, much like the infant, I would become emotionally upset, often resulting in tears. Even General George Patton, before PTSD was named and understood, recognized the disconnect when he said "The human mind, accustomed as it is to a certain discipline and order, is incapable of processing sudden change without trauma." As my brain rewires, those clashes or sudden changes become less frequent and / or less intense. None of this means I don't miss Dean or love him, because I do. I can still create the perfect storm of memories that will cause me sadness and tears, but it is only occasionally that I get "slapped upside the head" by grief.

So, what does this have to do with exercise? Maybe a lot.

Studies have shown that vigorous exercise can help mitigate the effects of some types of depression and mental illness as brain chemistry may be changed. Vigorous exercise is also related to longer telomere lengths, with athletes tending to have longer telomere lengths than non-athletes. Telomere length tends to shorten with age and may be associated with the risk of several age-related diseases. ** Studies have also shown that in some cases, where there is damage to the brain, the brain is capable of rewiring around the damaged portion. ***

*The Grieving Brain: The Surprising Science of How We Learn from Love and Loss, Mary-Frances O'Connor

**Choosing the Strong Path: Reversing the Downward Spiral of Aging, Fred Bartlit and Steven Droullard, along with Marni Boppart, M.D.

***Spark: The Revolutionary New Science of Exercise and the Brain, John J. Ratey, M.D. with Eric Hagerman

This makes me wonder if there might be a connection between vigorous exercise and "recovery" from grief. If moving on from grief involves the rewiring of the brain, and vigorous exercise impacts the brain's ability to rewire, does it not make sense that those involved in vigorous exercise before the trauma may be able to move on from or through grief more quickly because their brains rewire more efficiently? Or that those who begin to engage in vigorous exercise, as a way to deal with the loss, may hasten "recovery" as well? Of course, there is mindset of the person to consider. In my case, I was already focused, driven, resilient. No one ever accused me of being too sensitive or emotional. If anything, it was the opposite. Over and over, I've been told "You're the strongest person I know." Is it the personality, the vigorous exercise, some combination thereof? We may never have a clear answer. But for me, it makes sense, and that's what really matters.

It's Still Funny

No one, and I mean no one, could make me laugh the way Dean could. Tears running down my face, holding my stomach and braying like a donkey, or as Dean would say, "dunkey", while begging him to stop, just stop. He never would. He'd just keep going with his story until he couldn't hold it in and would just lose it. All he would have to do is say two words of the spiel, and I would lose it all over again.

I haven't laughed like that since he died, but I have laughed. Strangely enough, the most laughter has been connected to his death. I was at the gym and we were talking about my mother, who on her best days is just annoying, and I commented that Dean always said that she would outlive us all. The irony is not lost. We started saying that he is probably negotiating with the powers that be to, please, now that he is finally rid of her and can get some peace, keep her here. We were cracking ourselves up playing the different roles in the negotiation. Then, at lunch one day with some friends I said that I talk to Dean all the time but that he never answers. In perfect harmony, we all said "Just like when he was alive." One friend said he was going to stop responding to his wife, and when she asks why, he'll tell her that he's giving her practice for when he dies. It went on from there. The funniest, however, was the day he died. I got home from the hospital and, even on the worst day of my life, brought in the mail. Think about that for a second. Not only did I bring it in, I looked at it, and there, in all its "officialness" was a jury summons for Dean! I cracked up, immediately took a picture and sent it to a friend saying "Dean is laughing his ass off." My friend responded with "People will do a lot to avoid their civic duty." I laughed and laughed. It's still funny. Now that I think about it, maybe that's why Dean threw the damn spoon.

Death Changes Everything and Nothing

My old self died with Dean. My world shattered. The worst thing I never saw coming came with a vengeance. Strangely enough, the world didn't stop and still hasn't. It just keeps spinning like it always has. Friends and strangers just keep living their lives. A rat dies in the garage, the heat goes on the fritz, the bills still need to be paid. At least once a day, I look around and wonder "What the hell happened?" I want to scream at the world. "My husband died! My heart is broken! Don't' you care?" And, if the world answered truthfully, it would just say "No, don't care. That will be $39.95. Cash or card?"

I Thought I Would be Nicer

So many of the grief books talk about how the death of a loved one made them a kinder, gentler, more patient person. At first, I thought that might happen. Boy was I wrong. I think I've always, usually, more often than not, been a nice person. Patient and understanding, not so much. I think I'm still, usually, more often than not, a nice person. Patient and understanding, still not so much. In fact, even less than before, especially when it comes to whining or complaining about stupid shit. I think to myself, "Seriously? My husband is dead and you're upset because your coupon expired? Shut the fuck up and get out of my way!"

I'm more about me now. Not in a self-absorbed, I'm the only person that matters way. But I will no longer put myself out, rush through something, or to somewhere just to accommodate people who are not integral to my life. I'm more likely to speak up, say what I want and to hell with the rest of you. I don't go out of my way to be rude or mean; I avoid being either. I've just stopped caring what people who aren't important to me think. Whenever people would talk to Dean about what someone else thought about them or what they might say, his go to response was "Who gives a shit?" I'm picking up where he left off.

Falling in Love Again

For some reason, people keep bringing this up. Not people in general, but people who have been here or people who know someone who has been here. At some point, they say "You'll meet someone" and then proceed to tell you their own, their friend's, or family member's experience. Women seem to come in around the 4-year mark, men much sooner. Go figure. I assume the reason people want to tell me these stories is to provide some sort of comfort and hope for the future. They also counsel me that the person will have to understand, hence, so many people who have had spouses die connect with others who have experienced the same; they understand that you are two people, the before and the after. They understand that some days may be hard and to give you whatever it is you need, companionship or solitude. They understand that your love for your spouse will never die; they are secure enough to not try to or think they must compete with a ghost. One friend commented that when / if I'm interested, I need to find a younger man! She gave me two reasons. First, he has to be able to keep up with me, and second, based on life expectancy etc., I don't want to have to go through this shit again. I thought that was pretty funny. She may be right.

Right now though, I can't imagine loving another man. I can't imagine another man coming close to the man Dean was. Even so, I have fleeting thoughts of whether I will ever be happy or even have companionship. Part of me hopes the answer is yes. The other part agrees with my friend, I never want to go through this kind of pain again. Then, of course, there is the question of betrayal. What does it say about my love for Dean, if I can love someone else? I know the answer and that given the human capacity for love, one has nothing to do with the other. The best advice I have received and may someday take, is to be open to the possibility. As much as I hate hearing "Dean would want ...," I know that he wants me to be happy, and the only true betrayal would be to give up and not live my best life because that would be to dishonor our life together and everything he stood for. I know all of this, yet what I really want is our life together back. I also know that is the one thing I can't have.

At the Bottom of the Box

Although there are many interpretations and scholarly discussions about the myth of Pandora and the box (or the vase), gifted to her by Zeus, the prevailing one is that at the bottom of the box, hidden below all the evils and sorrows, was hope. No matter how bad things get when the furies are released, there is always hope for a better tomorrow. Bullshit. All I want is to get through today. I can't even think about tomorrow.

A Final Thought

As humans, we love to play "What if?" I'm not sure why because, for the most part, it's patently ridiculous, but we still do it. What if I had done this? What if Dean had done that? What if it had been me? At the time of Dean's death, I would have traded places with him in a heartbeat. He had so much left to give to this world, his talent, genius, friendship, and love. People and animals are less without him. His contribution to this world was and is so much more than mine will ever be. But, knowing what I know now, maybe that weird comment about it was better that it was Dean, had some bit of truth. To think he would suffer this pain is as unbearable as the pain itself. He was always more loving, patient and kind. He collected lost souls and understood them. For all his badassery, he felt things deeply. Of course he would have survived, just like I will, but knowing that wherever he is, afterlife, parallel universe, Blair Castle; he is happy and healthy, maybe even continuing his work, makes me think, when all was said and done, he's the lucky one.

Things I Didn't Mention

There are things I didn't mention that you may wonder about. I've heard people talk about the first time they came home to an empty house and the pain that brought. Dean was in the hospital for almost a month before he died, so I was somewhat used to coming home to an empty house. I have never felt lost in my house. If anything, it is a comfort to me to be surrounded by the home we built together, but I can certainly understand the other point of view. The other thing is wedding rings. Dean and I rarely wore our wedding rings. When I was working, I wore mine at work, but it came off as soon as I got home. Dean's work involved his hands on people or horses. We did wear them when we went out. My wedding and engagement rings belonged to Dean's mother, so they are family heirlooms. They are beautiful in their own right, so I will occasionally wear one or the other on my right hand. I know people who wear their rings on a chain. Others have said that when the time is right to take them off, you will know it.

Advice, Wanted or Otherwise

I think I've made it clear how I feel about a number of things related to how death and grief is treated in this world, so a list of dos and don'ts may seem redundant. However, there are a few things that I didn't address or that need to be highlighted, so here they are.

The Grieving Person

Don't be afraid to ask. I know you don't, for a myriad of reasons, want to ask, but you have to. In a way, you are driving this car. People, even your friends, don't know what to do. Unless they have experienced this grief, this is uncharted territory for them as well. But trust me, they want to help. In fact, they need to help. I let people take me to the airport. I asked people to help me move furniture. One friend practically begged me to give him a job. I finally gave in and agreed to let him clean out Dean's Westside office for me. I had only been there once, but I didn't want to do it, was dreading it. It had a finality to it that I just couldn't bear, so I finally said "yes." He was so grateful, and having that burden taken away was liberating. He took everything to his house, put it out on picnic tables, took photos and sent them to me. We were able to go through everything, and what I said I wanted, he brought to me. I then looked at those things and culled down further. What I didn't want, he took and donated. It made what would have been a traumatic experience into one that was tolerable. We even laughed.

Don't expect too much of people. Unfortunately, this is your grief. A part of your life has ended; theirs has not. You have irrevocably changed; they have not. There are no "Hallmark" moments. Busy-bodies? Insensitive? Can't read the room? No change there. Kind? Loving? Concerned? Fortunately, no change there either.

Another piece of advice I was given, but have not had a chance to use, is to, when necessary, "play the widow / widower card." I have been assured that it can be very effective in the right circumstance.

Supporting the Grieving Person

Many of the books I read encouraged people not to ask what the grieving person wanted and/or needed, but to just "take action." I disagree. Unless you really, really know the person, be very careful in assuming what they need or want and that they will be comfortable with you, essentially, invading their very private grief.

I do agree with the books regarding the "How are you doing?" questions, texts and calls. Especially in the early days, it was exhausting, because, as a polite person, I felt that I had to respond and this is where we get into the "ok" "getting by" and so on. A friend actually asked "How are you?" then stopped himself saying "That has got to be the stupidest question. I can't believe I said that" and we moved on. Other than that, the advice to "just do" and not make the person ask should be carefully considered. If you do want to reach out, a simple "I'm thinking of you" "I'm here for you" will go a long way. Just knowing that you are not forgotten is a comfort.

Don't make promises you can't keep. If you say "Whatever you need" "24/7", you better mean it. In other words, if you get a call at 2 a.m. "Please come, I need you," you had better be ready to jump in the car in your jammies and hit the road. Knowing that I had friends who really meant it, made it less likely that I would need them. (I never called anyone at 2 a.m. You're welcome.) Kind of like knowing that there is a safety net, makes you less likely to fall. If you can't promise everything, I recommend what one friend said "You can ask me for anything. I might not be able to do it, but if I can, I will."

Gifts and food are also tricky. I received gift cards from several people. I know they meant well. Unfortunately, some of them were for places I never go, and others were for places that I only went with Dean; just looking at them made me cry. So, again, unless you really know the person, be careful. It may be best to stick with generics. Food comes in two ways, through the "mail" or in person. Through the mail was fine, as it didn't require any personal interaction. I didn't get anything that made me think of Dean, but there is always that risk. I did get things that I don't eat. Some I gave away, some I threw away. I felt bad about that because I hate wasting food or money, so if you share those concerns, you should probably give some thought to sending food. Personal delivery brings it to a whole other level, part of which I will address in the next paragraph. Besides the whole, does the person even like it thing, there is the practical matter of the containers. Please do not bring food in containers that look like they should be returned (you know what I mean), or at least say, or include a note, that you don't need the containers back. This includes the containers carrying the containers, hot and cold carriers. Once I finished, in whatever way, the food, everything else went in the donation bag or in the trash. As much as I appreciated the gesture, because I knew what they represented, I couldn't stand to look at, let alone use, the containers.

My last piece of advice is the one I feel most strongly about. Unless this is your normal routine and/or the person has given you permission, DO NOT show up uninvited! You have no idea what is happening behind that door. Maybe they are eating, crying, having the first quiet moment of the day. The last thing I needed or wanted was someone, sometimes a complete stranger, showing up at my door. The first time it happened, as I was making my lunch no less, I was caught so off guard that I invited them in. It was awful. They asked questions, gave advice and got me so upset that by the time they left, I was ready to throw up. Even so, I felt bad that I hadn't offered refreshments! The next times it happened, I stood on the porch. I was polite, but I made it clear that my home was private, and I would not allow them to invade my space. In hindsight, I probably should have put up a sign that I was not entertaining visitors. In hindsight, it probably wouldn't have mattered.

The Wherefore

As I've said, I wanted this to be written to reflect the reality of my grief at the time. It has been tempting to go back and rewrite parts to reflect things I have learned or experienced, to make my language less offensive, to temper my anger, and, in some places, even be more serious. As I reach 8 months since Dean's death, my views on some things have changed, most have not. I still feel strongly that grief is war, and that we should call death what it is. My view on the things people say and do is the same. I haven't become more patient, kind or understanding. There is no transformation pending. What has changed is that I no longer hope to die. I'm still ok with it, but as the universe is clearly not going to cooperate, I've put that hope on the shelf. I'm still not leaping out of bed with joy of the new day, but then again, I never did that when Dean was alive. I have started, in a way, looking forward to things. Not with an "Only 2 more sleeps!" enthusiasm, but I look forward to meeting up with friends and trying new things. Speaking of which, I have added javelin and long jump to my track and field repertoire. Trust me, there is nothing like throwing a spear with everything you have to dispel anger and grief! There is also something to be said for running and then jumping through the air into a "sand box" to make you feel like a little kid. I laugh more. Not quite the Dean laugh until you cry, but I've laughed pretty hard. I don't think about Hope much because it is just evolving day by day. Every time I set a new goal or make a plan for the future, Hope peeks around the corner.

I still want to stab people who say "Time heals." Not because I disagree, but because there is more to it. The full saying is "Time heals all wounds." Think about it for a moment. Think about the different kinds of wounds. A scrape on your knee may heal without you doing anything. You get over someone being rude at the dentist without much fuss. But what about those wounds that require stitches or casts? Some wounds, such as amputations, are permanent. What differentiates the "healing" is how much work you have to put in. The bigger the wound, the more you have to participate in the recovery. Death of a spouse is one hell of a wound, and if you just let it fester, it will destroy you. You have to take care of you. It sounds trite, but you have to eat right, sleep more and get out and move. You have to be kind to yourself and show yourself grace. You can't win the war without being prepared in mind, body, and spirit.

At some point, however, how you respond to grief becomes a choice. In the early days, not so much. Right after Dean died, I couldn't have controlled my response to grief if my life depended on it, in which case, I would have succumbed with joy. That was then. This is now. I could easily allow grief to rule my days and passively wait for it to end, but I've chosen a different path, one where I can and do control my response to grief. This doesn't mean that I no longer get sad, I do. But when the sad comes, I choose whether to indulge it and for how long. I define my grief. It does not define me.

Most people are thrilled to see me taking control and working toward happiness. But, interestingly, some are not happy with my choices. They believe that I am "suppressing" and "denying." They believe that I should succumb to grief every time it rears its ugly head. Others express happiness but follow it with a warning, "That's great, but, you know, it will still hit you when you least expect it." Thanks so much for the support, I really need you to tell me that I'm an idiot and don't really understand what

I am experiencing. I know they think they are helping, but I as I've said over and over, ad nauseum, just stop it!

All of this said, do I still cry? Yes. Get angry? Yes. I have fragile days where I am terrified that I will forget Dean's voice, his look, his touch and that this will be some sort of indictment of my love for him. I hate that I will age while he will be frozen in time at 66. But, most of the time, life is somewhere between ok and pretty good, which is a hell of a lot better than where I started.

Acknowledgments

For Valerie Humphrey, thank you for saying "You have to write this now!" Without you, it wouldn't have happened.

For everyone who has supported and continues to support me through the worst thing I never saw coming. I thought I was tough, but this has brought me to my knees. Thank you for helping me to get back on my feet.

And most of all, for Stephanie Weissman. For once, I have no words. Actually, that's not true, I have three. I love you.

About the Author.

Jeanne Roy is a former prosecutor, who upon retiring from the law, jumped into the fitness world with both feet. She is a NASM Certified Personal Trainer with a specialization in Sports Performance Enhancement, a competitive sprinter, javelin thrower, long jumper, obstacle course racer and die-hard weight lifter. She loves teaching and showing older adults how to stay healthy and strong so that they can do whatever it is they want to do. She is the author of *Spike Up! Becoming an Athlete at 60*. This is her second book; one she never wanted to write.

www.ingramcontent.com/pod-product-compliance
Lightning Source LLC
Chambersburg PA
CBHW040726120726
48010CB00001B/29

* 9 7 9 8 2 1 8 4 1 5 6 8 6 *